Emergency Jobs

Military Personnel

by Julie Murray

Dash!
LEVELED READERS
An Imprint of Abdo Zoom • abdobooks.com

2

Level 1 – Beginning
Short and simple sentences with familiar words or patterns for children who are beginning to understand how letters and sounds go together.

Level 2 – Emerging
Longer words and sentences with more complex language patterns for readers who are practicing common words and letter sounds.

Level 3 – Transitional
More developed language and vocabulary for readers who are becoming more independent.

THIS BOOK CONTAINS RECYCLED MATERIALS

abdobooks.com

Published by Abdo Zoom, a division of ABDO, PO Box 398166, Minneapolis, Minnesota 55439.
Copyright © 2021 by Abdo Consulting Group, Inc. International copyrights reserved in all countries.
No part of this book may be reproduced in any form without written permission from the publisher.
Dash!™ is a trademark and logo of Abdo Zoom.

Printed in the United States of America, North Mankato, Minnesota.
102020
012021

Photo Credits: Getty Images, US Air Force, US Air National Guard, US Army, US Marines Corps, Shutterstock, ©US Army p.cover / CC BY 2.0
Production Contributors: Kenny Abdo, Jennie Forsberg, Grace Hansen, John Hansen
Design Contributors: Dorothy Toth, Neil Klinepier, Laura Graphenteen

Library of Congress Control Number: 2020910915

Publisher's Cataloging in Publication Data

Names: Murray, Julie, author.
Title: Military personnel / by Julie Murray
Description: Minneapolis, Minnesota : Abdo Zoom, 2021 | Series: Emergency jobs | Includes online resources and index.
Identifiers: ISBN 9781098223076 (lib. bdg.) | ISBN 9781098223779 (ebook) | ISBN 9781098224127 (Read-to-Me ebook)
Subjects: LCSH: Soldiers--Juvenile literature. | Military personnel--Juvenile literature. | Military service members--Juvenile literature. | Assistance in emergencies--Juvenile literature.
Classification: DDC 363.3481--dc23

Table of Contents

Military Personnel

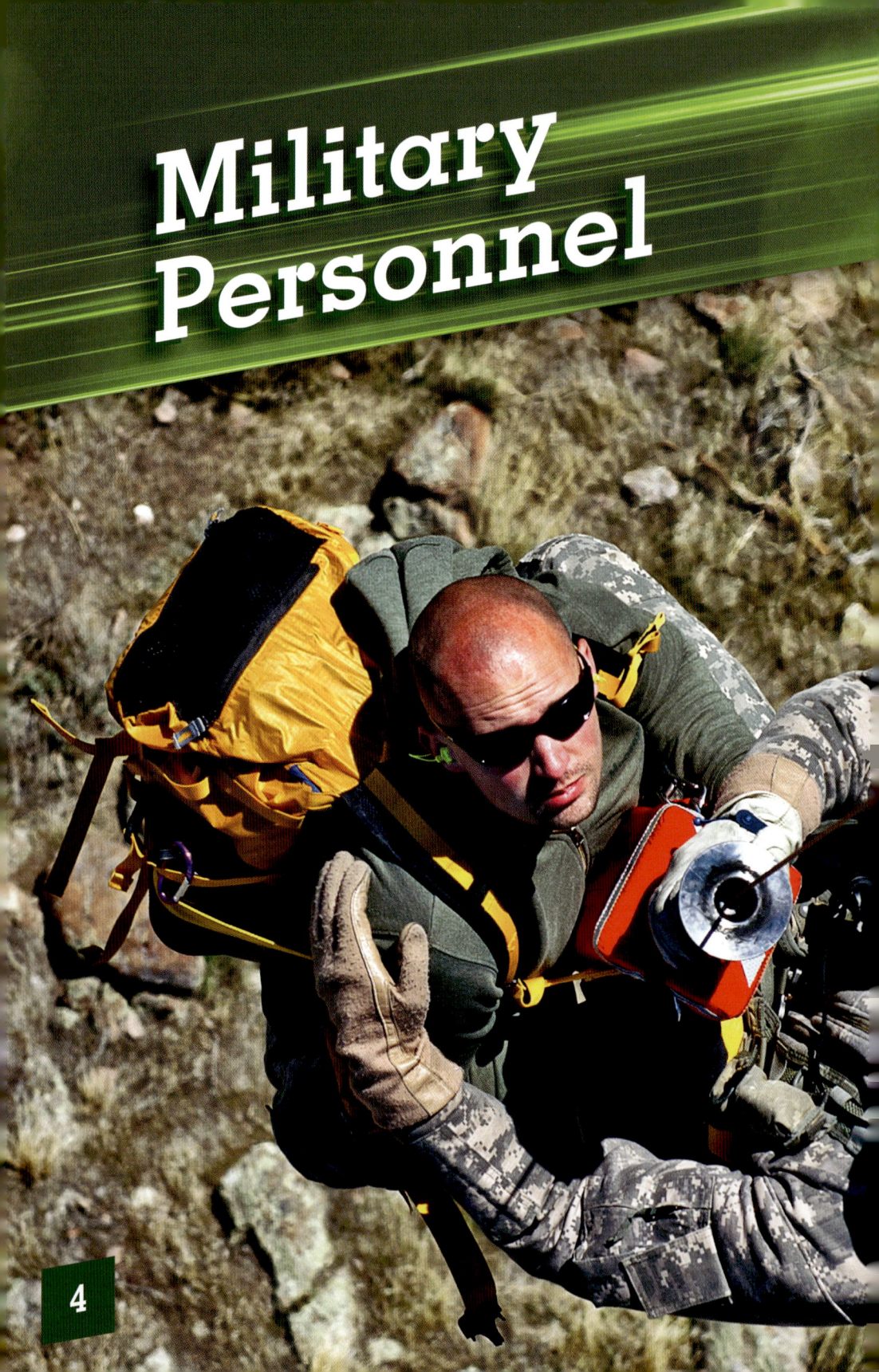

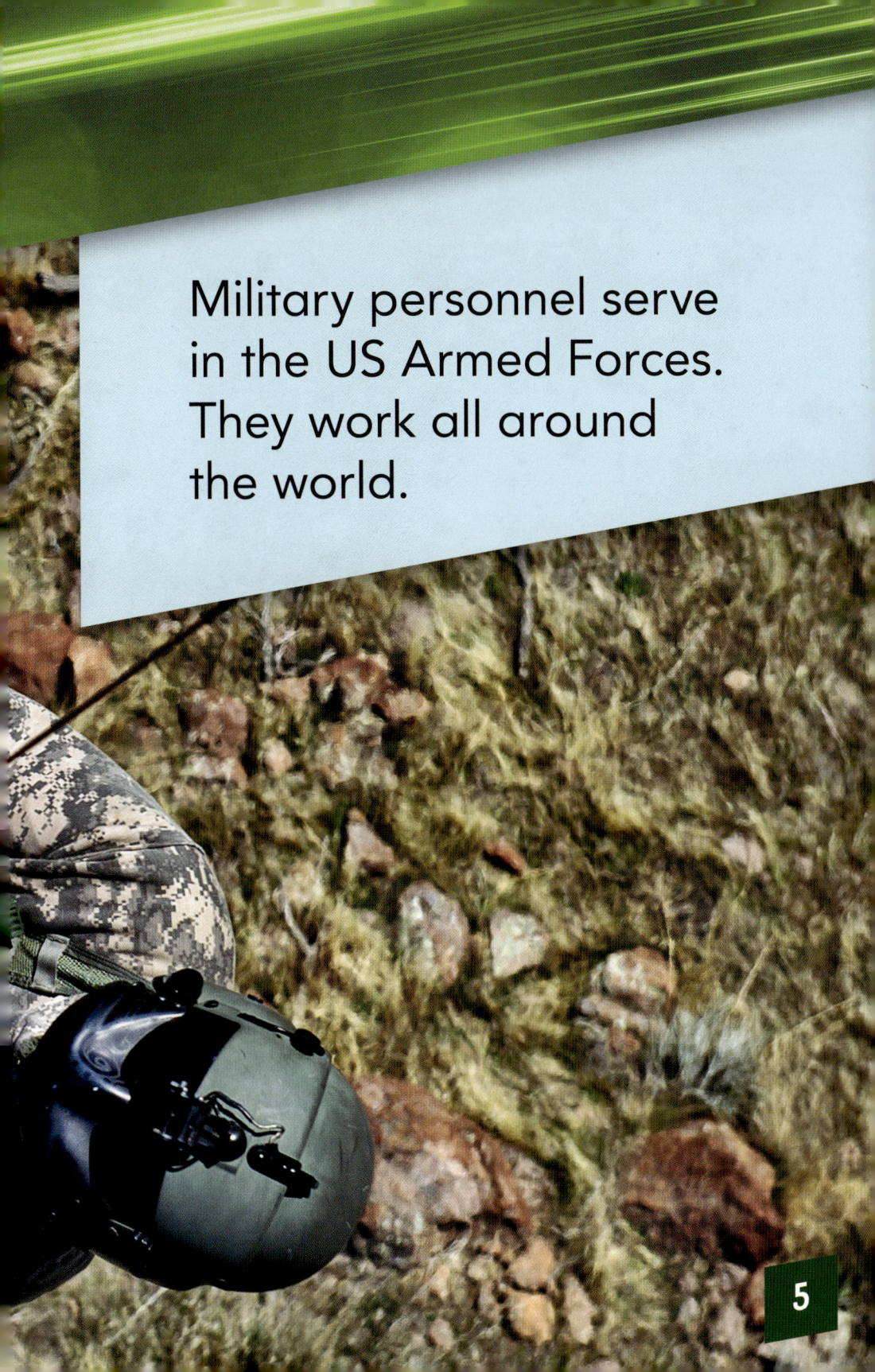

Military personnel serve in the US Armed Forces. They work all around the world.

Their job is to protect the US and its citizens.

Military personnel work in many emergency situations. There are lots of different jobs.

Jobs

Combat medics help injured soldiers. They treat those **wounded** during battle.

Pararescuemen jump out of airplanes. They parachute down. They rescue injured soldiers.

Military personnel do helicopter water rescues. They pull people from the water and bring them to safety.

The military also helps during national emergencies. They set up testing sites during **COVID-19**.

The military helps during **natural disasters** too. They go on search and rescue missions. They also deliver supplies.

Military personnel do more than just go to battle. They protect and serve in many ways.

More Facts

- There are more than 1 million active military personnel in the United States.

- Active US military members work in 150 different countries.

- The Army is the largest US military branch. It has more than 471,000 members.

Glossary

COVID-19 – short for Coronavirus Disease 2019, the illness caused by a certain coronavirus. People who have the illness often experience a cough, fever, and shortness of breath. Some people require treatment from a doctor.

natural disaster – a natural event such as a flood, earthquake, or hurricane that causes great damage or loss of life.

wounded – injured.

Index

Online Resources

Booklinks
NONFICTION NETWORK
FREE! ONLINE NONFICTION RESOURCES

To learn more about military personnel, please visit **abdobooklinks.com** or scan this QR code. These links are routinely monitored and updated to provide the most current information available.